Guyana

French Guiana

Suriname

ATLANTIC OCEAN

Mouth of the River Amazon

You've made it!

Stayed with very friendly river people

9 oo

10 ew

11 ue

Saw beautiful parrots and pink dolphins

Amazon River Basin

Largest river basin and greatest rainforest on Earth

Brazil

Brazilian Highlands

ai

a | a–e | ai

Snail Train

By Sara

Read the words.

Set 1 (9 words)	Set 2 (20 words)	Set 3 (20 words)	Set 4 (20 words)	Set 5 (20 words)
snail	certain	tail	maize	waiting
train	straight	rail	jailed	brainy
rain	paint	paid	failure	prepaid
exclaimed	wait	jail	maintain	complaint
pain	raise	bait	raising	drainage
explain	main	trail	sustain	monorail
complain	sail	aid	traitor	faithfully
waiting	claim	frail	dainty	daintily
again	gain	praise	waiter	remainder
9 words so far	faith	bail	curtain	remaining
	fail	saint	raisin	container
	against	brain	restrain	retraining
	contain	waist	aimless	aimlessly
	remain	drain	fountain	maintenance
	captain	faint	detained	praiseworthy
	detail	stain	refrain	uncomplaining
	afraid	chain	waitress	sustainable
	mountain	strain	saintly	disdainfully
	bargain	slain	trainers	obtainable
	nail	Spain	claiming	unobtainable
	29 words so far	49 words so far	69 words so far	89 words so far

up to 39 Sparking	40–49 Glowing	50–59 Burning	60–69 Sizzling	70+ Red hot!
Score/Date				
Score/Date				

One Minute Wonders

4

Read the limerick then draw the picture.

Poor Snail Train was stuck in the rain
And exclaimed to himself, "What a pain!
I will need to explain
Before people complain
About waiting around once again!"

Practise writing.

Build your word power.

Brilliant! You are off!

Well done!
ue
ew
oo
ow
oa
-y
igh
ea
ee
ay
ai

You have pulled your fast water kayaks high up into the Andes Mountains of Peru, arriving at the source of the Apurimac River, the longest tributary of the River Amazon. It is just a puddle of water! You paddle aimlessly through the first section of 740 km, beginning with tiny ankle-deep creeks that turn into canyons 3 km deep and only 90 m wide! When there are very dangerous rapids, you need to carry your kayaks around them. The terrifying Acobamba Abyss claims to be one of the most dangerous whitewater stretches in the world.

ay

a | a–e | ai | ay

Mayday! Mayday!

By Fran

Read the words.

Set 1 (11 words)	Set 2 (20 words)	Set 3 (20 words)	Set 4 (20 words)	Set 5 (20 words)
may	**way**	strayed	portray	swaying
day	**say**	bray	braying	Domesday
bay	**says**	clay	display	prepay
dismay	**play**	played	crayfish	waylay
spray	**stay**	fray	layer	holiday
swayed	**lay**	plays	fairway	runaway
stayed	**pay**	days	delayed	takeaway
prayed	**away**	frayed	railway	hideaway
okay	**always**	sprays	displays	replaying
midday	**today**	trays	straying	caraway
ray	**maybe**	sprayed	betrayed	portrayal
11 words so far	**yesterday**	prayer	dismayed	repaying
	pray	delay	essay	delaying
	sway	crayon	stingray	holidays
	jay	repay	playwright	bayonet
	slay	ashtray	displayed	flyaway
	stray	subway	array	betrayal
	tray	decay	birthday	portrayals
	splay	dismay	runway	takeaways
	slayed	delays	mislay	holidaying
	31 words so far	51 words so far	71 words so far	91 words so far

up to 39 Sparking	40–49 Glowing	50–59 Burning	60–69 Sizzling	70+ Red hot!
Score/Date				
Score/Date				

Read the story then draw the picture.

"Mayday! Mayday! Mayday!"
We looked out into the bay in dismay because there in the spray swayed a ship. We stayed and prayed that it would be okay. At midday, a ray of sunshine burst out and very soon everyone was rescued.

Practise writing.

Build your word power.

Brilliant! You made it to the next stage!

Well done!
- ue
- ew
- oo
- ow
- oa
- -y
- igh
- ea
- ee
- ay
- ai

You have survived the Powac rapid which marks the end of the whitewater section, and from here on the water is flat for the next 6115 km to the Atlantic Ocean. You move all your gear into giant flat water kayaks. The next stage is called the Red Zone. It is very dangerous so you have to radio ahead to the villages on the river banks to tell them you are coming to stay or they might think you are bandits! The river is wider but still fast flowing. You stay at Iquitos, the largest town in the world without a road leading to it.

ee

e | e-e | ee

Cheesy Feet

By Bella

Read the words.

Set 1 (10 words)	Set 2 (20 words)	Set 3 (20 words)	Set 4 (20 words)	Set 5 (20 words)
sleepy	see	agree	Greeks	beeline
teenager	been	succeed	tweet	weekly
knees	need	degree	breed	fleeting
sweets	free	committee	sleet	sleeveless
between	seen	jeep	flee	creeping
teeth	tree	speech	fleet	discreet
screeched	seem	peep	beech	decree
reek	feel	keen	fee	seething
cheesy	week	deed	asleep	bootee
feet	street	weed	beetle	disagree
10 words so far	green	peel	cheeky	proceeding
	meet	sleeve	toffee	refugee
	deep	screen	unfreeze	beefeater
	wheels	sweep	cheetah	agreement
	feed	sweet	creepy	chimpanzee
	sleep	cheese	coffee	succeeded
	speed	creep	keenly	guarantee
	keep	bleed	feeble	absentee
	steel	cheek	greeted	agreeable
	indeed	greed	greedy	disagreement
	30 words so far	50 words so far	70 words so far	90 words so far

One Minute Wonders

	up to 39 Sparking	40–49 Glowing	50–59 Burning	60–69 Sizzling	70+ Red hot!
Score/Date					
Score/Date					

Read the story then draw the picture.

The sleepy teenager had muddy knees and sticky sweets between his teeth.
"But worst of all," his mother screeched, "you reek of cheesy feet!"

Practise writing.

Build your word power.

Well done!
ue
ew
oo
ow
oa
-y
igh
ea
ee
ay
ai

Brilliant! You made it to the next stage!

You have paddled the Colombian stretch of the river and reach the point where the borders between Columbia, Peru and Brazil meet. After your passport is stamped at a small riverside camp, you are off into Brazil, travelling deep in the Amazon Rainforest. There are 2,500,000 types of insects, including mosquitos that give you malaria. You have to wear trousers, long-sleeved shirts and lots of insect repellent. It is over 35 degrees and the sun is very strong out on the water so you must wear a hat and lots of sunscreen.

ea

e | e-e | ee | ea

Eat the Teacher

By Freddie

Read the words.

Set 1 (12 words)	Set 2 (20 words)	Set 3 (20 words)	Set 4 (20 words)	Set 5 (20 words)
teacher	each	steal	wreath	conceal
beach	leave	real	clean	beaver
reading	read	repeat	heath	appeal
tea	speak	beneath	feat	decrease
heat	beat	disease	creak	feature
sea	clean	really	weave	meagre
meaty	please	season	teak	mistreat
feast	team	reason	teal	weasel
eat	east	creature	squeal	mislead
mean	reach	increase	peal	preheat
screamed	stream	breathe	preacher	overeat
seal	seat	peat	queasy	reasoning
12 words so far	dream	wheat	teaspoon	leadership
	weak	bleach	repeat	featureless
	peace	peach	teaming	misleading
	teach	lean	cleanest	decreasing
	reached	leap	pleading	overeager
	least	peak	meanwhile	reasonable
	easy	squeak	squeaky	unspeakable
	deal	bean	beagle	unreasonable
	32 words so far	52 words so far	72 words so far	92 words so far

	up to 39 Sparking	40–49 Glowing	50–59 Burning	60–69 Sizzling	70+ Red hot!
Score/Date					
Score/Date					

One Minute Wonders

10

Read the story then draw the picture.

The teacher sat on the beach reading her book and having tea. Because of the heat, she went to swim in the sea.
"Ah! A meaty feast for me to eat!" said the shark.
"Don't be so mean!" screamed the seal.

Practise writing.

Build your word power.

Well done!
ue
ew
oo
ow
oa
-y
igh
ea
ee
ay
ai

Brilliant! You made it to the next stage!

4

There was a huge tropical rainstorm this afternoon. It rains every day because the River Amazon is on the Equator. In some places they have nearly 200 cm of rain a year and the river floods so much that it can be 190 km wide. You reach a village where the houses float on logs. The reason is so that when the floods come up the houses float up with the water! Locals use their boats to catch fish and to visit their neighbours. When you leave, you have to be careful of the caimans as you step into the canoe.

11

Sizzling Syllables! 1

Read the syllables.

Five syllable types so far

Closed	fan	fren	sim	lon	trun	rip	lat	rim	tol	stom
Open	fra	de	lo	pri	bu	fre	bi	na	ve	cu
Evil e	ane	ete	ile	ome	ule	ale	epe	ise	oze	upe
-r	mar	stor	ver	orth	lar	ther	ard	der	for	art
-le	-gle	-zle	-dle	-cle	-fle	-kle	-tle	-ple	-ble	-sle

Got it? ☐

***Paddle the Amazon* patterns**

gai	cay	eep	ain	tee	clea	trai
cree	eal	tray	feeb	lay	ead	cray
spray	feat	tain	rea	gree	plai	slee
rai	way	scree	eat	bray	real	dai

Got it? ☐

Prefixes and suffixes

-ing	mis-	re-	dis-	-al	im-	-ful
-ment	inter-	de-	-est	non-	-y	-ed
pre-	-ness	-ity	pro-	-ly	il-	un-
-en	sub-	-er	-less	semi-	-able	be-
trans-	-ous	-ic	fore-	non-	over-	under-

Got it? ☐

Fiery Phrases! 1

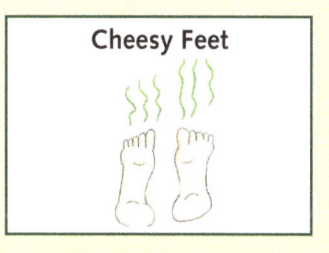

Snail Train

Mayday! Mayday!

Cheesy Feet

Eat the Teacher

Read the phrases.

Set 1	Set 2	Set 3
stay and play	meet and greet	he seemed to be afraid
wait and see	have some tea	put on your trainers
take the train	on the beach	over the heath
sail away	fast asleep	a screech of wheels
raise the flag	what a treat	raise your hand
to his dismay	look and see	he appealed to the teacher
the first chain	feel the beat	what a great feast
paint a picture	don't scream	the best team ever
today is the day	turn up the heat	he ate greedily
an important saint	up the stream	the cheeky teenager
until the rain comes	below the peak	clean your teeth
he started to pray	something easy	sweep up now
drain the sink	eat a peach	lean on me
no pain, no gain	reached the beach	take a peek
straight away	he started to scream	she agreed to speak
take aim	teaming with fish	display all your work
once again	what a feat	peaches and cream
above the snail	read every word	across the plain
take the strain	a few leaves	two young waiters
going on holiday	take a seat	maybe I can stay
20 phrases	20 phrases	20 phrases

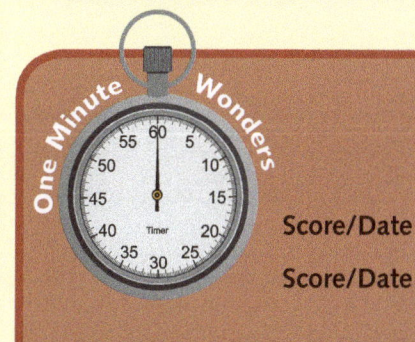

	up to 29 Sparking	30–39 Glowing	40–49 Burning	50–59 Sizzling	60+ Red hot!
Score/Date					
Score/Date					

13

igh

i | i-e | igh

Mighty Knight

By Sebastian

Read the words.

Set 1 (10 words)	Set 2 (15 words)	Set 3 (15 words)	Set 4 (15 words)	Set 5 (15 words)
bright	**right**	tightest	slightly	higher
night	**high**	upright	eyesight	lightening
mighty	**fright**	knighted	lightbulb	frightening
knight	**slight**	airtight	blighted	mightier
thighs	**light**	brighten	sighing	almighty
fight	height	brightness	fighter	delightful
might	tight	daylight	lightness	oversight
alright	flight	tightly	frightful	enlighten
lightning	sigh	brightened	highest	mightiest
sight	blight	brighter	brightly	unsightly
	rights	fighting	slighter	frightfully
	sighs	frightened	sprightly	candlelight
	sighed	delight	brightest	enlightened
	tighter	lighter	flightless	firefighter
	lightened	tightened	fortnight	delightfully
10 words so far	25 words so far	40 words so far	55 words so far	70 words so far

One Minute Wonders

up to 39 Sparking	40–49 Glowing	50–59 Burning	60–69 Sizzling	70+ Red hot!
Score/Date				
Score/Date				

Read the story then draw the picture.

One bright moonlit night the mighty knight, with tree trunk thighs, came out to fight. He might have been alright but when lightning struck, boy what a sight!

Practise writing.

Build your word power.

Brilliant! You made it to the next stage!

Well done!
ue
ew
oo
ow
oa
-y
igh
ea
ee
ay
ai

Because of the storm, the river is high and running incredibly fast. Paddling is very difficult as you get caught up in whirlpools and currents. You get a fright as there are lots of things floating near you, including big logs which might damage your boat. Your hands are blistered and your muscles are aching from all the hours of paddling you have done. Tonight the village you stay in has houses on stilts. You are welcomed by the sight of a little boy carrying a baby armadillo in his arms.

-y

| i | i-e | igh | y |

My Spy Fly

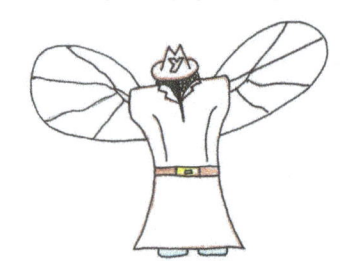

By Fred

Read the words.

Set 1 (11 words)	Set 2 (16 words)	Set 3 (17 words)	Set 4 (18 words)	Set 5 (18 words)
my	**by**	shyly	qualify	signify
spy	**cry**	prying	replying	amplify
fly	**why**	trying	butterfly	complying
sly	**dry**	crying	dragonfly	applying
sky	**July**	buying	satisfy	replying
pry	**reply**	dryly	horrify	resupply
shy	**supply**	spying	classify	retrying
apply	occupy	drying	mystify	mystifying
rely	sty	comply	justify	satisfying
buy	ply	flytrap	terrify	multiplying
try	retry	greenfly	multiply	resupplying
11 words so far	ally	relying	glorify	preoccupy
	defy	denying	sanctify	terrifying
	deny	defying	mollify	horrifying
	flying	reapply	stupefy	justifying
	slyly	supplying	verify	glorifying
	27 words so far	simplify	rectify	classifying
		44 words so far	highflyer	simplifying
			62 words so far	80 words so far

One Minute Wonders

up to 39 Sparking	40–49 Glowing	50–59 Burning	60–69 Sizzling	70+ Red hot!
Score/Date				
Score/Date				

16

Read the story then draw the picture.

My spy fly is very sly. He can go up into the sky and pry into every house. He is not shy and will apply himself to any job so I can rely on him! I won't let you buy him even if you try!

Practise writing.

Build your word power.

Well done!
ue
ew
oo
ow
oa
-y
igh
ea
ee
ay
ai

Brilliant! You made it to the next stage!

6

As there is no village, you sling your hammock between two trees with a cover to keep you dry overnight, and climb in. It is very difficult to sleep as the animals, birds and insects of the forest make so much noise. Try not to step on a snake or scorpion if you need to get out in the night! You must also stick close to the camp because although they are shy, you know there are jaguars about because you heard the alarm call of a howler monkey. Jaguars, the biggest cats in South America, are very dangerous but you hardly ever see them.

17

oa

o | o-e | oa

Stoat in a Coat

By Mariana

Read the words.

Set 1 (11 words)	Set 2 (20 words)	Set 3 (20 words)	Set 4 (20 words)	Set 5 (20 words)
stoat	**coast**	goat	coastal	roasted
floated	**road**	poach	boater	floated
moat	boast	gloat	coasted	armloads
boat	cloak	loan	goalie	charcoal
toad	soap	oat	houseboat	meatloaf
speedboat	croak	load	loaded	coastguard
boasting	toast	coax	loafer	cockroach
whoa	foal	roam	coaster	cloakroom
groaned	coach	hoax	floating	croaky
soaked	moat	oath	approach	encroach
coat	loaf	roach	toadstool	coaxing
11 words so far	foam	loathe	soapy	toasted
	roast	broach	presoak	goalposts
	soak	moaned	boastful	loathsome
	float	coaxed	poaching	scapegoat
	oak	roamed	roaming	goalkeeper
	moan	loathed	coastline	boastfully
	goal	loaned	boasted	encroaching
	shoal	poached	groaning	approachable
	coal	croaked	toadstools	unapproachable
	31 words so far	51 words so far	71 words so far	91 words so far

up to 39 Sparking	40–49 Glowing	50–59 Burning	60–69 Sizzling	70+ Red hot!
Score/Date				
Score/Date				

Read the story then draw the picture.

The stoat floated round the moat in his little boat. A toad whizzed by in his flashy speedboat boasting, "Look how fast I can go!"
"Whoa!" groaned the stoat. "You have soaked my smart new coat!"

Practise writing.

Build your word power.

Brilliant! You made it to the next stage!

Well done!

| ue |
| ew |
| oo |
| ow |
| oa |
| -y |
| igh |
| ea |
| ee |
| ay |
| ai |

The river is so wide now that you can't see the other side. There are no roads through the forest so everyone uses boats to get around. There are ferries that travel for days between towns and villages. Be careful not to float into their path as you would get soaked or overturned by their wake. As you approach the river bank you spy a capybara, which is very exciting! It's another night in a hammock trying not to think of the 2 m anaconda or shoal of piranhas that might be swimming in the river close by.

19

ow

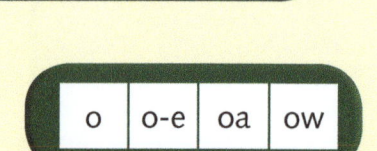

o | o-e | oa | ow

Glow in the Snow

By Edward

Read the words.

Set 1 (11 words)	Set 2 (20 words)	Set 3 (20 words)	Set 4 (20 words)	Set 5 (20 words)
below	**show**	bowed	pillow	unknown
window	**grow**	blown	bellow	followed
own	**slow**	flown	fellow	slower
snowman	**shown**	mowed	fallow	regrow
bow	**known**	mown	sallow	bellowed
blow	**flow**	thrown	meadow	disowned
grow	**low**	grown	owner	widow
yellow	**owe**	sown	grower	overblown
glow	**throw**	flowed	bowler	stowaway
know	**follow**	rowed	elbow	overthrow
snow	**narrow**	mowed	grown-up	borrowing
11 words so far	**shadow**	borrow	crowbar	marshmallow
	tomorrow	sorrow	disown	billowing
	mow	harrow	owing	bellowing
	row	arrow	mower	narrowing
	tow	barrow	lowly	elbowing
	bowl	burrow	bowling	lowering
	grows	furrow	knowing	bungalow
	sow	shallow	rower	wheelbarrow
	stow	hollow	lower	overshadow
	31 words so far	51 words so far	71 words so far	91 words so far

up to 39 Sparking	40–49 Glowing	50–59 Burning	60–69 Sizzling	70+ Red hot!
Score/Date				
Score/Date				

Read the story then draw the picture.

Below my window I could see my very own snowman wearing his bright blue bow tie. The wind began to blow and suddenly my snowman started to grow and a yellow glow surrounded him! I needed to know what that glow in the snow could be …

Practise writing.

Build your word power.

Well done!
ue
ew
oo
ow
oa
-y
igh
ea
ee
ay
ai

Brilliant! You made it to the next stage!

8

You reach the confluence with the River Negro. Negro means black and for 6 km the river flows with two colours before the brown water of the Amazon mixes with the black water of the Negro. There is a big change tonight as you stay in Manaus, which is the largest city in the Amazon. It was once the richest in the world because the inhabitants grew so many rubber trees there. You haven't seen a city for weeks so it is very exciting to be shown around, sleep in a proper bed and have supper in a restaurant.

21

Sizzling Syllables! 2

Read the syllables.

Row the Atlantic review

fab	ell	sta	ife	ess	ti	itch
etch	fle	iff	ple	chil	arf	mu
war	ese	den	gra	atch	ate	uzz
fer	cu	orb	ack	-gle	met	cle
une	otch	-zle	co	ope	wor	utch

Got it? ☐

New *Paddle the Amazon* patterns

might	oad	stow	spy	cry	oach	high
by	dow	tight	oaf	fright	bow	try
low	fly	oam	own	ply	oax	row
sight	oast	fy	light	oal	ny	right

Got it? ☐

All *Paddle the Amazon* so far

spray	feat	tain	rea	gree	plai	slee
rain	way	eech	peat	bray	real	dain
low	fly	oam	own	ply	oax	row
sight	oast	fy	light	oal	ny	right

Got it? ☐

Fiery Phrases! 2

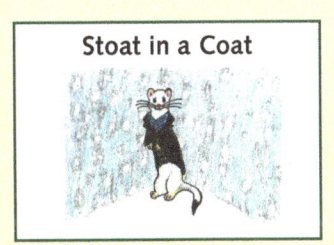

Mighty Knight

My Spy Fly

Stoat in a Coat

Glow in the Snow

Read the phrases.

Set 1	Set 2	Set 3
in the sky	it gave me a fright	see you tomorrow
late July	my thigh is hurting	throw that ball
tell me why	the sky is brightening	below the window
it is dry	a heavy load	slower than ever
in the night	watch the road	mind your elbow
what a fright	a loaf of bread	you have grown
a bright light	I love roast beef	a great bowler
it's brighter now	moan and groan	a narrow path
what a sight	don't gloat	too slow
you are right	I like to eat toast	blow out the candle
higher than ever	look at the toad	look at the snow
it can fly	a load of coal	go slowly
please don't cry	what a lovely foal	follow me
buy it now	take an oath	the shallow end
don't be shy	go to the coast	put it in this bowl
let's not fight	float on the moat	row the boat
a mighty knight	take my coat	tie a bow
the highest mountain	a coastal path	four soft pillows
turn off the light	get on the coach	the rabbit burrow
it's too bright	warm and toasty	swallow this
20 phrases	20 phrases	20 phrases

	up to 29 Sparking	30–39 Glowing	40–49 Burning	50–59 Sizzling	60+ Red hot!
Score/Date					
Score/Date					

23

oo

Goose in Boots

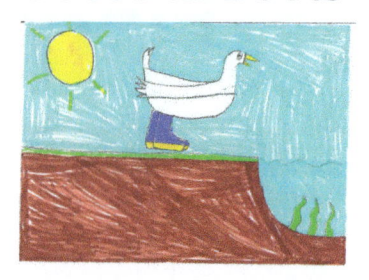

By Edward

| u | u-e | oo |

Read the words.

Set 1 (11 words)	Set 2 (19 words)	Set 3 (20 words)	Set 4 (20 words)	Set 5 (20 words)
foolish	**too**	roof	noodles	smoothness
goose	**room**	boost	scooter	smoothly
boots	**choose**	gloom	doodle	aloof
hooligan	**food**	groove	saloon	shampoo
school	**soon**	boom	toothless	bamboo
pool	**proof**	snooze	foolproof	taboo
cool	**shoot**	bloom	cocoon	cuckoo
kangaroo	tool	tooth	schooner	tattoo
loose	moon	stoop	platoon	igloo
maroon	mood	loot	shooting	yahoo
balloon	ooze	drool	harpoon	kazoo
	hoot	noon	doodling	bamboozle
	smooth	hoop	lagoon	foolishly
	moose	spoon	choosy	gooseberry
	fool	scoop	oodles	moodily
	spool	hooves	stooping	gloomily
	roost	noodle	tooting	foolishness
	hoof	rooster	snooping	cockatoo
	zoo	poodle	gloomy	didgeridoo
		cartoon	moody	hullabaloo

11 words so far
30 words so far
50 words so far
70 words so far
90 words so far

up to 39 Sparking	40–49 Glowing	50–59 Burning	60–69 Sizzling	70+ Red hot!
Score/Date				
Score/Date				

One Minute Wonders

Read the story then draw the picture.

The foolish goose in boots ran like a hooligan around the school pool. It was so cool! The next moment he bumped into a kangaroo who was on the loose with a maroon balloon. POP!

Practise writing.

Build your word power.

Well done!
ue
ew
oo
ow
oa
-y
igh
ea
ee
ay
ai

Brilliant! You made it to the next stage!

9

After weeks of paddling, you feel weary and gloomy as you still have more than 1500 km to go to the sea. To boost your mood, you just think of it as one day at a time. Because the river is so enormous now, you see huge ocean-going ships taking cargo from all over the world to Manaus. You spend the night with an indigenous Indian tribe in their wonderful house called a shabono. They paint your face the same as theirs and you soon join in, eating their food and dancing.

ew

u | u-e | oo | ew

Crew in a Stew

By William

Read the words.

Set 1 (9 words)	Set 2 (16 words)	Set 3 (17 words)	Set 4 (17 words)	Set 5 (17 words)
few	**new**	hew	curfew	unscrewing
crew	**grew**	brewed	renew	chewier
stew	**view**	crews	newish	newspaper
chewy	**blew**	hewed	steward	reviewing
flew	screw	ewes	unscrewed	jewellery
threw	drew	strewn	preview	chewable
knew	ewe	chewed	corkscrew	newsworthy
cashews	news	nephew	crewcut	renewing
brew	yew	review	reviewed	brewery
9 words so far	dew	unscrew	skewer	newscaster
	pew	renewed	hewing	newlywed
	mew	viewing	mewing	chewiest
	stewed	brewer	askew	newsagent
	shrew	chewing	Jewish	interview
	skew	newborn	curlew	unchewable
	jewels	dewdrop	bejewelled	renewable
	25 words so far	dewy	mildew	interviewing
		42 words so far	59 words so far	76 words so far

One Minute Wonders

up to 39 Sparking	40–49 Glowing	50–59 Burning	60–69 Sizzling	70+ Red hot!
Score/Date				
Score/Date				

Read the story then draw the picture.

When a few of the crew were put in the stew, the cannibals found them too chewy and flew into a terrible rage. They threw the stew away in disgust. They knew they would only have cashews left to eat now so they poured themselves a wicked brew!

Practise writing.

Build your word power.

Well done!
ue
ew
oo
ow
oa
-y
igh
ea
ee
ay
ai

Brilliant! You made it to the next stage!

10

More weeks of exhausting paddling in the boiling sun and sometimes you are actually sick from the heat and tiredness. Parrots flew over this morning and you have seen incredible pink dolphins playing near the boat and a few huge manatees lounging around. You are still 160 km from the sea but the tide comes this far up the river and makes a huge wave called a bore, so you have to be very careful. When you hear news of one coming, you keep away from the bank where the wave is at its highest.

ue

| u | u-e | oo | ew | ue |

Superglue Sue

By Kelly

Read the words.

Set 1 (11 words)	Set 2 (14 words)	Set 3 (15 words)	Set 4 (15 words)
Tuesday	**due**	venue	retinue
blue	**argue**	rescued	avenues
valuable	**value**	subdue	barbecues
statue	**continued**	issue	arguing
avenue	continue	virtue	rescuing
clue	queue	ensue	barbecue
Superglue	rue	revue	misconstrue
Sue	flue	issued	statuesque
rescue	hue	valued	misconstrued
tissue	cue	statues	revenue
true	fuel	issues	arguable
11 words so far	cruel	ensued	overdue
	gruel	pursue	issuing
	duel	subdued	undervalue
	25 words so far	pursued	valuation
		40 words so far	55 words so far

	up to 39 Sparking	40–49 Glowing	50–59 Burning	60–69 Sizzling	70+ Red hot!
Score/Date					
Score/Date					

Read the story then draw the picture.

It was Tuesday and Tim was feeling blue. His valuable little statue lay on the avenue in bits and he didn't have a clue how to mend it.
Superglue Sue to the rescue! She handed Tim a tissue and said, "Don't cry! I will make it perfect once again. Believe me, it's true."

Practise writing.

Build your word power.

Well done!
ue
ew
oo
ow
oa
-y
igh
ea
ee
ay
ai

Brilliant! You've done it!

11

You have paddled 6440 km in seven months and have reached the mouth of the River Amazon at Belem without needing to be rescued! The Atlantic Ocean is ahead of you and it is true that the estuary is 330 km wide! You have a barbecue on the beach to celebrate and remember all the wonderful things you have seen. You want to tell everyone the value of the great Amazon Rainforest; how many thousands of species live there and how important it is for the whole planet, changing carbon dioxide into oxygen for us to breathe.

Sizzling Syllables! 3

Read the syllables.

New *Paddle the Amazon* patterns

oos	few	sue	crew	view	clue	chew
jew	cue	oot	lue	tue	kew	gloo
snoo	rue	phew	strue	scoo	drew	due

Got it? ☐

Paddle the Amazon mix-up

row	gree	stoa	might	toon	dry	floa	spy
ait	new	sue	stow	cay	rew	strain	row
fright	rea	ail	own	croa	boo	gloo	feeb
crew	low	brew	spee	strue	stray	cray	view
proo	ply	light	oax	main	quea	sight	spea
bay	cue	wea	fy	flow	mew	eech	lue

Got it? ☐

WordBlaze so far

nai	oal	wa	eak	par	mow
ibe	for	igh	oom	tay	atch
tew	wor	ell	mai	fy	fer
gar	rue	gloa	orm	uke	cry
oop	lay	ter	war	eem	war
fee	pu	own	uss	rew	nue
fly	cue	eave	roak	wo	row
utch	wor	py	ight	ead	iff

Got it? ☐

Fiery Phrases! 3

Goose in Boots

Crew in a Stew

Superglue Sue

Read the phrases. Do you remember all the spelling patterns you have learnt so far?

Set 1	Set 2	Set 3
take this spoon	I knew it	a big statue
choose a balloon	he drew a picture	they are arguing
have a snooze	eat your stew	give me a tissue
enjoy the pool	it's too chewy	please don't argue
it's so cool	I like cashews	it's due today
a gloomy day	the winning crew	continue on
look at the kangaroo	a new car	I haven't a clue
don't be foolish	turn the screw	a long avenue
go to school	she threw it away	it's not true
in the mood	in the news	come to the rescue
I want some food	dew on the grass	when is it due
there's no room	review your work	a very long queue
don't be choosy	three large jewels	it is a bargain
at noon	the yew tree	my dog has strayed
in the loop	chew your meat	I disagree
watch this cartoon	the bird flew off	we all want peace
take the loot	the wind blew	my eyesight is good
in the groove	he is her nephew	please retry
a loose end	renew your library book	roaming around
we're going soon	the view was beautiful	the bellowing bull
20 phrases	20 phrases	20 phrases

	up to 29 Sparking	30–39 Glowing	40–49 Burning	50–59 Sizzling	60+ Red hot!
Score/Date					
Score/Date					

31

Blazing Extras

Read the words.

al	el	il
The Musical Medal by Flora	Travel by Camel by Beth	Pupil in Peril by Lily

Set 1		Set 2	Set 3
metal	actual	**travel**	**evil**
local	material	**level**	council
equal	occasional	parcel	pencil
usual	individual	angel	fossil
practical	plural	excel	nostril
several	natural	towel	devil
political	normal	camel	Brazil
general	sandal	tunnel	until
animal	musical	squirrel	pupil
capital	logical	tinsel	daffodil
magical	digital	label	daredevil
arrival	oval	channel	peril
canal	fatal	rebel	tendril
final	central	novel	utensil
pedal	hospital	level	vigil
total	medical	cruel	gerbil
medal	abysmal	vowel	civil
petal	additional	chapel	stencil
		cancel	lentil
36 words		19 words	19 words

Never use -le ➡ if you need a soft **c** or soft **g**.
➡ after these red letters: **N**igel • **u**sually • **r**ides • **m**ucky • **w**hite • **v**ans!

32

High frequency words not in patterns

are	long	move	think	put
the	sure	one	idea	pull
do	said	once	ask	even
two	have	here	last	along
to	than	there	were	want
too	any	their	don't	past
into	many	your	only	friend
off	some	four	often	because
of	come	does	listen	colour
you	they	ago	our	people

Question words

- what
- where
- why
- when
- which
- who

Beginning with be

begin	belong
before	beside
become	between
behind	beneath
below	began

a before l or ll

all	also	talk
call	always	walk
hall	almost	stalk
wall	alright	chalk
small	already	mall
ball	although	altogether

o u little devil

- would
- could
- should

By Clementine

33

🔥 White Hot Wonder! 🔥

Read the words.

Set 1	Set 2	Set 3	Set 4
certain	view	cleanest	runaway
reach	roast	newsagent	foolishly
groaned	sleepy	complaint	upright
holiday	chewy	highest	feeble
apply	queue	replying	goalkeeper
choose	explain	delayed	classify
disagree	occupy	approach	unobtainable
below	tightly	shallow	leadership
bright	moaned	greedier	lowering
rescue	swayed	value	chewier
remain	slowly	concealed	prayer
coast	increase	interviewing	doodling
supply	newish	faithfully	sprightly
screamed	argue	mystify	horrify
smooth	flow	mightiest	boastfully
display	against	borrowing	chimpanzee
continue	satisfy	succeed	disowned
known	breathe	loathed	avenue
speech	frightened	betrayal	misleading
sight	foaming	snooze	renewed
20 words	20 words	20 words	20 words

Beat your time!

Set 1	Set 2	Sets 1 and 2

Set 3	Set 4	Sets 3 and 4